There are soooo many playgrounds here! Some were big, were epic and some were boring. We explored all **70 playgrounds in Arlington County, Virginia** (not including school playgrounds) on the weekends between April-July 2015.

Since kids are very busy, we reviewed every playground so you can make the most of your play time! If you see us at the playground, tell us how you like our guide. -- **Avery and Spencer**, Arlington Science Focus School

(Warning: This guide contains the candid and sometimes immature opinions of two elementary school kids. It is inappropriate for adults. -- Dad)

Avery is 9 years old and entering 4th grade. She likes climbing equipment -- especially monkey bars -- and any kind of spinny-majigs. She enjoys reading and doodling too.

We used a star system to rate each playground

* = Bad
** = O.K.
*** = Good
**** = Great!
***** = Epic!!!!

Spencer is 6 years old and entering 1st grade. He likes swings and digging for worms. He also likes tube slides and monkey bars.

Avery's Picks

Chestnut Hills
Fillmore
Ft. Barnard
Ft. Scott
Parkhurst
Penrose
Rocky Run

Spencer's Picks

Chestnut Hills
Drew
Fairlington
Ft. Barnard
Ft. Scott
Glebe
Glencarlyn
Highview
Parkhurst
Westover

Dad's Favorites

Chestnut Hills
Fairlington
Ft. Barnard
Glencarlyn
Parkhurst
Penrose
Rocky Run
Woodlawn

Alcova Heights

Spencer: I like the river and jungle gym.★★
Avery: Tire swing, shady, big. ★★★

Dad: Very shady with zip line and stream nearby.★★★

Arlington Hall West

Spencer: Loved the rocks for looking for worms! ★★★
Avery: Colorful. ★★

Dad: Swings with zip line and covered picnic table

Arlington Mill

Spencer: Love the pirate ship. ***
Avery: Small, for pre-school. **

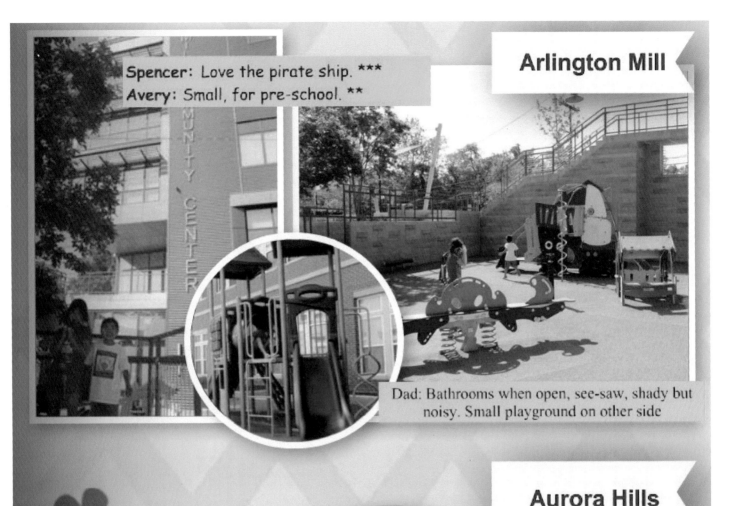

Dad: Bathrooms when open, see-saw, shady but noisy. Small playground on other side

Aurora Hills

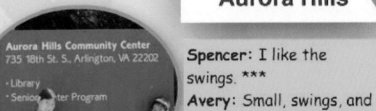

Aurora Hills Community Center
735 18th St. S., Arlington, VA 22202

• Library
• Senior Center Program

ARLINGTON

Spencer: I like the swings. ***
Avery: Small, swings, and volleyball. Lots of climbing equipment, colorful. ***

Dad: Shady with bathroom

Bailey's Branch

Spencer: I like the swings and jungle gym. The swings made me go the highest I ever went on a swing. ***

Avery: Stream, shady, lots of birds, small. *

Dad: Small place with swings

Bannekar

Spencer: I love this place. Fun swings and awesome jungle gym. Sandbox. ****

Avery: Swings, climbing eqp, bridge/stream. **

Dad: Quiet neighborhood park surrounded by homes.

Barcroft

Dad: Giant sports complex with bathrooms

Spencer: Really good climbing equipment. **
Avery: Nets for climbing, shade, spinning chair, see-saw. ***

Big Walnut

Welcome to
Big Walnut
Park

Spencer: This place is pretty cool. I like the slide. ****
Avery: Climbing eqp, sandbox, spinny- majig. ***

Dad: 1 covered table, small, quiet, see saw, spin table

Bluemont

Spencer: I love the train and the climbing rocks. ***
Avery: Awesome, really cool. Huge and fun. Cool train, swings sand box and bars. ****

Dad: Nice train theme, shady with bathroom.***

Bon Air

Spencer: Fun playground. Adventure ship. I like everything. ***
Avery: Ship shape, garden, we saw a wedding couple taking pictures! ***

Dad: Nice gardens but small. Don't confuse with smaller playground on lower level

Butler Holmes

Spencer: Only like the climbing. ***
Avery: Climbing, sort of empty, hot! **

Dad: Cool climbing net, covered picnic tables, swings

Carlin Hall

Spencer: Kinda boring. **
Avery: Small, garden, old, cemetery. **

Dad: Next to Glencarlyn library and community garden. Charming white house with bathroom, peaceful, swings, picnic table under shady tree ***

Charles Stewart

Dad: One covered picnic table, shady

Spencer: I do not like this place. There's blood in the tunnel and it's boring. *
Avery: Tunnel, slides, and sandbox **

Cherrydale

Dad: Shady, tall trees. Small, quiet, hidden but old equipment

Spencer: I don't like anything. *
Avery: I like how it is kind of secret from most people but it was cozy and shady. **

Spencer: I love this place. I will not leave. *****
Avery: Swings, slides. *****

Dad: One of largest w/swings and zip line. Shady, separate pre-school area with modern eqp, porta-john. ****

Clarenford Station

Spencer: Really don't like spinny thingy majigy. *
Avery: LOVE! I fell in love with this place! (mostly because of the spinny-majig). ***

Dad: Noisy with Route 66 next door.

Dawson Terrace

Spencer: Cool and a little bit stupendous. ***
Avery: Yay! No worms! This is pretty good. *

Dad: Older, next to wood trail, swings

Doctor's Run

Spencer: I don't like anything except
the sandbox. ***
Avery: Kind of for little kids.
Reeeeeeeeeeeeeeealy ooooooooold **

Dad: Shady, tall trees, swings,
several jungle gyms, zip line

Douglas

Spencer: I don't like anything except the swings. ***
Avery: I loved the swings in the sandbox. ***

Dad: Covered table, 2 sets of swings. Quiet neighborhood, lots of green with bridge/stream nearby

Drew

Spencer: Amazing big red climbing thing and wobbly shapes for stepping on. *****
Avery: Bouncy jumping items, slide swings, no shade, climbing structures, two playgrounds. ****

Dad: Sprayground, new equipment, swings, no shade

Eads

Spencer: I love this place. Everything is so fun and it is so peaceful. ****

Avery: Large, lots of climbing equipment, colorful (lots of yellow), lots of slides. ****

Dad: Decent size next to an open field

Edison

Spencer: Everything is really small except the swings. *

Avery: Ok, Swings are fun. Smallish. *

Dad: Only one jungle gym but quiet with swings

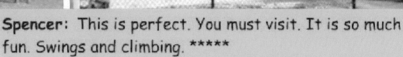

Spencer: This is perfect. You must visit. It is so much fun. Swings and climbing. *****

Avery: Slides, climbing structures, swings, no color. ***

Dad: Very large playground with swings & bathroom

Fillmore

Spencer: Awesome! Love a lot of stuff. ****

Avery: I will leave it a surprise for you! *****

Dad: OK, older equipment. Kids liked it

Fort Barnard

Spencer: I love everything and the pine tree. *****
Avery: I loved everything especially the spinning nets to climb. It was kind of like High View but much awesomer! *****

Dad: new and big with swings and fort *****

Fort Ethan Allen

Spencer: This place is good. Nice and shady. Also nice zipline. ***
Avery: Boring boring boring boring zipline. **

Dad: Zip line, swings, next to Madison comm. ctr, quiet. Dog park next door

Fort Myer Heights

Spencer: I like the tree trunk thing and the secret passage. I also like the swings. ★★★

Avery: Looks like wood. Fun turf grass. ★★★

Dad: Small but newly-renovated

Fort Scott

Dad: Older, but kids enjoyed it. Has bathroom, swings

Spencer: This is so much fun. There's roller slides and high slides. ★★★★★

Avery: Large, ages 6-12, lots of eqp, baby park + big kids park, swings, creative slides, ladders and bridges, picnic tables, colorful, tennis ct, basketball and baseball ★★★★★

Foxcroft Heights

Spencer: Really small. **
Avery: Small, shady, nearby a cemetery. *

Dad: Tiny but shady, views of Washington

Glebe Road

Spencer: I like the peaceful park with swings and a bridge that goes over a brook and at the end of the bridge there are paths for hiking. *****
Avery: There are 6 swings. THAT'S ALL THERE WAS (plus a tennis court) ***

Dad: No playground, just swings, next to Gulf Branch. Very shady with stream

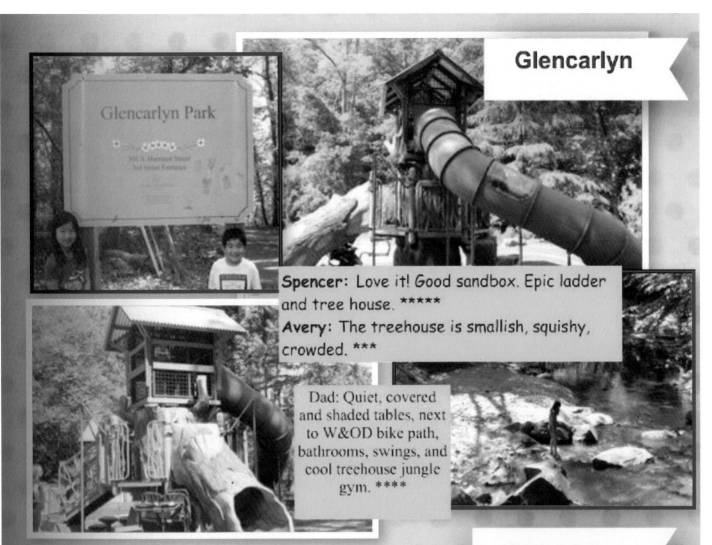

Glencarlyn

Glencarlyn Park

Spencer: Love it! Good sandbox. Epic ladder and tree house. *****

Avery: The treehouse is smallish, squishy, crowded. ***

Dad: Quiet, covered and shaded tables, next to W&OD bike path, bathrooms, swings, and cool treehouse jungle gym. ****

Gunston

Middle School
Community Center
Theaters
Athletic Facilities

Spencer: This place is not really fun. *
Avery: Medium size, extra bars, colorful, high, zipline. ***

Dad: Older eqp., zipline, bathroom

Hayes

Spencer: Llllooovvvveeee the swings.
That's all I can say! ★★★
Avery: It's cool. Pretty big and fun. ★★★★

Dad: sprayground, bathroom, covered picnic
tables, swings, very large area

Henry Clay

Henry Clay Park

3011 7th Street North, Arlington, VA 22201

Spencer: I love it. I had so much
fun breathing on my sister
through the speakers. ★★★
Avery: It's pretty cool. The
slides are GREAT! ★★★

Dad: Neighborhood park surrounded by
homes, zip line. covered table

Henry Wright

Dad: small, just one structure

Welcome to
Henry Wright
Park

Spencer: Very boring. Only like see-saw. ★★
Avery: okay...sort of babyish.   See-saw is ok. ★★

High View

Welcome to
High View
Park

Dad: Quiet, bathrooms, climb wall, swings, covered table, zip line needs lube. ★★★

Spencer: I love the water play area and slide. They are so much fun. ★★★★★
Avery: Spinny majig, rock climbing, window-slide, zipline, swings. ★★★★

Jennie Dean

Spencer: Rapid fun. Good sliding bars. ****
Avery: Awesome slanted double bar, swings, sandbox, small. **

Dad: Shady with swings

Lacey Woods

Spencer: Awesome. I loved everything. Good sandbox, slides and zipline. ****
Avery: Swings, woods, climbing structure, sandbox field. **

Dad: Bathrooms, zip line, shelter with picnic tables

Langston-Brown

Spencer: Has epic thing called strawberry cottage. I like everything. ***

Avery: I like the underground bench. *

Dad: Old eqp., needs upgrade, swings

Lee

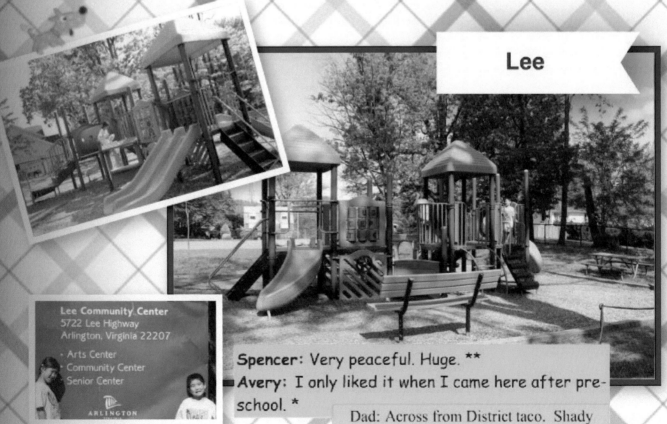

Lee Community Center
5722 Lee Highway
Arlington, Virginia 22207

- Arts Center
- Community Center
- Senior Center

ARLINGTON

Spencer: Very peaceful. Huge. **

Avery: I only liked it when I came here after pre-school. *

Dad: Across from District taco. Shady

Lubber Run Comm. Ctr.

Spencer: Small but good for rainy days. ***
Avery: It is not a playground*

Dad: An indoor playground good for rainy or cold weather

Lubber Run Park

Spencer: Really boring. Only sandbox. **
Avery: SHADY, BIG! ***

Dad: Big, swings covered table, Connected to big park.

Lyon Village

Spencer: Kinda fun. I know how to turn on the sprayground. **
Avery: For little kids but fun. Picnic tables under gazebo

Dad: Shady neighborhood playground with covered picnic tables, swings and sprayground.

Madison

Spencer: I do not like the look of it. It is boring and hot. *
Avery: For little kids. *

Dad: For toddlers. Next to Ft. Ethan Allen

Madison Manor

Spencer: This place is so fun. Nice sand playing area. ★★★★
Avery: Swings, sandbox, slides. ★★★

Dad: Bathroom, swings, covered picnic tables, massive sandbox, shady

Maury

Spencer: Awesome ship, lots of spinning things. ★★★
Avery: Really small. The top part is REALLY scary. It creaks with loud noises plus it's high but the spinning teacup is fun. ★★

Dad: Behind Arlington Arts Ctr. Small & quirky

Dad: Small neighborhood place. Shady w/ swings

Spencer: Very small. Don't like it. *
Avery: Blech. Excuse me, but my brother just put millions of worms on the slide. Sooo, yeah, that was a bad experience. *

Monroe

Spencer: I don't like anything except the swings. **
Avery: Boring. Did I mention it was really boring? No stars.

Dad: Quiet w/swings. Better for for pre-school

Mosaic

Spencer: Very small, little net and big climbing wall. **

Avery: Can get very hot, challenging to climb.**

Dad: New eqp, no shade, near Ballston restaurants

Nauck

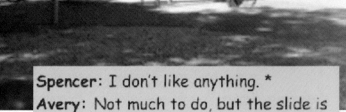

Spencer: I don't like anything. *

Avery: Not much to do, but the slide is really awesome. **

Dad: New, bathrooms, small, quiet, steep slide

Nelly Custis

Spencer: I like the slides and monkey bars. Slide is nice and swirly. Monkey bars are nice and high. **

Avery: Medium size, swings, benches (lots), extra space, picnic tables, shade. **

Dad: swings, quiet, residential, near Nina Park

Nina

Spencer: I really do not like it. It is too babyish. *

Avery: Baby toys, not fun. **

Dad: For toddlers, quiet, residential, near Nelly Custis Park

Oakgrove

Under renovation

Welcome to
**Oakgrove
Park**

Parkhurst

AMAZING

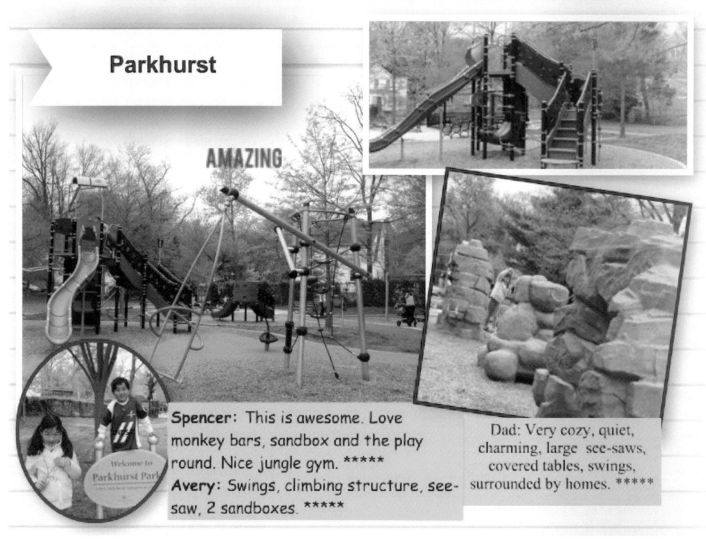

Spencer: This is awesome. Love monkey bars, sandbox and the play round. Nice jungle gym. *****

Avery: Swings, climbing structure, see-saw, 2 sandboxes. *****

Dad: Very cozy, quiet, charming, large see-saws, covered tables, swings, surrounded by homes. *****

Penrose

Spencer: Awesome slide. Nice jungle gym. ****
Avery: Cool! This is a really big but not shady. It was super hot but it was worth it. *****

Dad: Well designed, nice, pre-school section, swings, climbing wall, covered tables. *****

Quincy

Spencer: This place is boring. Sometimes I think it's a little cuckoo. **
Avery: Small, zipline, monkey bars, hook, volleyball, library. **

Quincy Park
1021 N. Quincy St.

Dad: Zip line, volleyball, shady, bathroom in nearby library, covered tables

Rocky Run

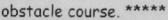

Spencer: I have been here a billion times. It is fun and it has a big climbing net. ****

Avery: Giant spider web, new swings, other obstacle course. *****

Dad: Newly renovated. and challenging climbing eqp. Covered tables, bathrooms, swings, fields, toddler area, partly shady. *****

Rosslyn Highlands

Spencer: Nothing much to do. *

Avery: Ok, smallish, pretty colorful. **

Dad: Small, older eqp.

Slater

Spencer: I don't like this place. Nothing to do. *
Avery: 0 stars

Dad: The smallest playground in the county. Not much to do

Thomas Jefferson

Spencer: Big jungle gym. Really awesome shady thing. ***
Avery: Bouncy thing. **

Dad: Cool balance beam

Towers

Spencer: I only like sandbox. *

Avery: Small but the sandbox was the best part. *

Dad: One of the smallest playgrounds

Troy

Spencer: This is sorta fun but the cool part about it is the flowing stream. . ***

Avery: Colorful, no climbing eqp, small, swings. **

Dad: Small but has swings

Tuckahoe

TUCKAHOE PARK
2400 SYCAMORE ST.

Dad: Big place w/swings, climbing net

Spencer: I like this place, there are fun climbing ropes. ****
Avery: Climbing eqp., Spinning-majig, see saw, ropes. ****

Tyrol

Spencer: Not very fun. Nothing to do. . **

Avery: Spiny-awesome-majig. Otherwise old, rusty and small. . **

Dad: Access to Long Branch. Covered tables w/swings but old eqp.

Virginia Highlands

Virginia Highlands Park
1600 South Hayes Street
Aurora Hills Library & Recreation Center
Senior Adult Center

ARLINGTON

Spencer: I like the monkey bars. I do not like the other stuff like the high wobbly bars and the slide because it's too short. The high slide is good. ★★★

Avery: Very small, lots of trees, not for 9+, did I say it was small? ★★

Dad: Older eqp. but shady

Walter Reed

Welcome to Walter Reed Playground

Spencer: I like the music machine and jungle gym. ★★★

Avery: It was fine but kind of boring. There was a sandbox and a seesaw and musical metal chairs and table. They were very loud. The climbing thing was actually really hard to climb across. ★★

Dad: New, bathroom in community ctr, metal drums, see-saw, but no shade

Westover

Spencer: Awesome places to play and sorda cool slides. Also like the swings. *****

Avery: Climbing structures, swings and box, rock climbing. ****

Dad: Picnic shelter, bathroom, swings, next to 66 so a little noisy

Woodlawn

Spencer: b-o-r-i-n-g Only like sandbox and swings. Didn't like everything else. **

Avery: I liked the sandbox. I liked the swings. Didn't like the stuff (that is short for things) ***

Dad: Cute, large place encircled by homes. Swings, stream, shady with multiple play eqp. *****

Woodmont

Dad: xylophone, covered table but overhead planes. Next to YMCA

Spencer: Nice xylophone, boring jungle gym. ***
Avery: I didn't like that the best part was blocked off for repairs. I am awesome! I liked the bells. **

Woodstock

Under renovation

Woodstock Park
2049 North Woodstock St.

List your favorite playgrounds:

We are fortunate to live in a county with so many playgrounds. This was a fun adventure. We were surprised that the kids and parents did not always agree on the best and worst playgrounds,

We have donated a few copies of this guide to the Arlington County Library. If you would like a personal copy for yourself or for a gift, please contact: hkpark100@hotmail.com

CPSIA information can be obtained at www.ICGtesting.com
Printed in the USA
BVIW12n2104200416
445001BV00013B/87